'TWAS THE KNITS BEFORE CHRISTMAS

'TWAS THE KNITS BEFORE CHRISTMAS

Fiona Goble

Ivy Press

First published in the UK in 2011 by
Ivy Press
210 High Street
Lewes
East Sussex BN7 2NS
United Kingdom
www.ivypress.co.uk

British Library Cataloguing-in-Publication Data
A catalogue record for this book is available from the British Library

ISBN: 978-1-907332-91-3

This book was conceived, designed and produced by
Ivy Press
Creative Director *Peter Bridgewater*
Publisher *Jason Hook*
Editorial Director *Tom Kitch*
Senior Designer *James Lawrence*
Designer *Megan Parkin*
Illustrator *Clemency Bunn*
Photographer *Neal Grundy*

Printed in China

Colour origination by Ivy Press Reprographics

10 9 8 7 6 5 4 3 2 1

Contents

Introduction

The magic of Christmas makes it probably most children's favorite time of the year, as they dream of Santa Claus racing across the sky in his sleigh to deliver their presents (if they have been good, of course), just as Clement Clarke Moore described in 'Twas the Night Before Christmas.

This book features ten knitting projects that have been inspired by the poem, including a St. Nicholas doll, eight reindeer which children will fall in love with, and a life-size stocking that can be hung up on Christmas Eve. If you're an inexperienced knitter you may wish to look at the basic techniques section before you get started.

In the bag

Before you get knitting, first check that you have all the things you need. Realizing that you're missing something when you're halfway through a project is no fun at all! If you've knitted several projects before, you'll probably have everything you need. But it's always worth checking through the list just in case. Most of the items are reasonably priced and available from knitting or craft stores.

Knitting needles

Most of the projects in this book are knitted using size 2/3 (3 mm) standard knitting needles. For some of the projects, you will also need standard knitting needles in the following sizes: 3 (3.25 mm), 2 (2.75 mm), and 1 (2.25 mm). The particular sizes of needles you need for each project are listed in the patterns themselves.

Crochet hook

While the patterns do not involve crochet as such, a crochet hook in size D-3 (3.25 mm) is used to create crochet chains that are used for some of the dolls' hair, hanging loops, and a small number of other details. Full instructions are given within the patterns. If you already have a crochet hook of a similar but not identical size, this will be fine and you won't need to buy a new one.

A needle to sew your work together

You will need a sewing needle with a large eye and a fairly blunt end to sew your items together. Sometimes these needles are called yarn needles, but a tapestry or darning needle will work just as well.

Embroidery needle

You will need an embroidery needle, with a sufficiently large eye to thread through a length of double knitting (DK) yarn, to embroider the dolls' features and some other items. These needles have more pointed ends than tapestry or darning needles, enabling you to get between the strands of your yarn, which is essential for some of the embroidery stitches.

Standard sewing needle

You will need an ordinary sewing needle to sew on some of the embellishments in the projects, such as buttons and bows.

Watersoluble pen

This is useful to mark the position of the dolls' features before you embroider them. It is also useful to copy some of the designs onto your knitting before you embroider them. Watersoluble pens are like ordinary felt pens, but the ink disappears when sprayed or dabbed with water. The ink is safe to use on almost all yarns and fabrics, but it is always worth testing it in an inconspicuous area to make absolutely sure.

Small safety pins

These are used to hold spare knitting stitches while you are working on a separate area of the project. You can also use small safety pins instead of threads, to mark certain rows in your knitting.

Pair of compasses and an ordinary pencil

You will need these to draw the wreath shape (see page 62) on your foam board.

Craft knife

You will need this to cut out your wreath shape from your foam board.

Red coloring pencil

This is used to color some of the dolls' cheeks and St. Nicholas's nose (see page 54).

Small scissors

A small pair of sharp scissors is essential for trimming yarn tails without the risk of snipping your knitting.

Tape measure

You will need this to check the length of your crochet chains and to measure certain parts of your knitting when you are piecing your projects together. You may also need it to measure your yarns.

Dressmaking pins

You might find ordinary dressmaking pins helpful to pin your project pieces together before sewing them.

Row counter

You can buy different kinds of row counters, from simple plastic ones that fit on the end of a knitting needle to electronic devices that hang round your neck. They are not as necessary for small knitting projects such as those within this book as they might be for larger items such as garments. Nevertheless, some knitters do find that they come in handy.

More than a good yarn

To make the projects in this book you will need a selection of standard double knitting (DK) yarn and a few other types of yarn. Double knitting yarn is slightly finer than a worsted-weight yarn. You will also need some other materials, all of which are included in this round-up.

Yarns

The main parts of all the projects in the book are knitted in standard DK yarns. We recommend that you use 100% wool yarns or yarns that contain at least 20% wool. Yarns made from 100% acrylic or 100% cotton do not have the natural stretch and pile of woolen yarns and do not produce such attractive or professional-looking results.

For some of the projects you will also need a cream mohair yarn, a fluffy white textured yarn of similar weight to DK yarn, and gold crochet yarn, all of which you should be able to find in your regular knitting store.

Embroidery floss

For a small number of projects you will need embroidery floss in various colors. These can be metallic, rayon, or cotton. The floss you choose will affect the look of your finished project.

Standard sewing thread

You will need this to sew decorations such as buttons and bows on some of your projects. You can also use it as a thread marker to mark the beginning and end of specified rows of your knitting.

Polyester filling

This is a soft fluffy filling made from 100% polyester that is specially made to stuff toys and other handmade items. It is widely available in craft stores. Make sure that the one you choose conforms with all relevant safety standards.

Foam board

Foam board (sometimes called foam core) consists of a layer of Styrofoam, coated on both sides with paper. It is lightweight and rigid. The foam board used for the wreath (see page 62) should be approximately ¼ in/5 mm thick. Foam board is available in most art and craft shops.

ABBREVIATIONS

YOU WILL FIND THE FOLLOWING ABBREVIATIONS IN THIS BOOK:

K knit

P purl

st(s) stitch(es)

st st stockinette stitch (alternate rows of knit and purl stitches—see page 13)

beg beginning

k2tog knit the next two stitches together

p2tog purl the next two stitches together

kwise by knitting the stitch or stitches

pwise by purling the stitch or stitches

inc1 increase one stitch by knitting into the front and then the back of the next stitch

m1 make one stitch by picking up the horizontal loop before the next stitch and knitting into the back of it

sl1 or **sl2** slip one or two stitch(es) by slipping onto the right-hand needle without knitting it/them

psso pass slipped stitch over by passing the slipped stitch over the stitch just knitted

ssk slip, slip, knit by slipping two stitches one at a time, kwise, then knitting the slipped stitches together

yo yarn over (take your yarn over the needle to the other side)

f front

b back

rs right side

ws wrong side

cont continue

rem remaining

rep repeat

g gram(s)

oz ounce(s)

mm millimeter(s)

cm centimeter(s)

in inch(es)

m meter(s)

yd(s) yard(s)

Gauge

The knitting gauge for the patterns in this book is 12 sts and 16 rows to 1½ in/4 cm square or 32 sts and 42 rows to 4 in/10 cm square over st st on size 2/3 (3 mm) needles.

The gauge when knitting small items like the ones in this book is not as crucial as when you are knitting clothes. The main thing is to make sure that your knitting is quite firm, so that your items keep their shape and the stuffing does not show through your knitted fabric. However, if you knit unusually tightly, you may want to use slightly larger needles than those recommended. If you knit loosely, you may want to choose slightly smaller knitting needles.

Knitting know-how

All knitting stitches are made up from just two basic stitches—the knit stitch and the purl stitch. And of course you'll also need to know how to cast on and bind off. If you're new to knitting or want to brush up your skills, grab yourself a ball of yarn and a pair of knitting needles and follow the instructions below.

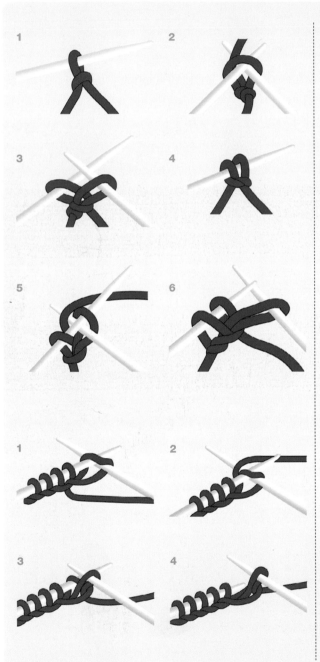

Casting on

1 / Make a slip knot by making a simple loop of yarn and pulling another loop of yarn through it. Put your needle through the loop and pull the slip knot up quite firmly. This slip knot is your first cast-on stitch.

2 / To make the next cast-on stitch, hold the needle with the slip knot in your left hand. Insert the point of your right-hand needle through the slip knot from left to right. Then wind your yarn around the needle tip.

3 / Use the tip of your needle to pull a loop of yarn through the first cast-on stitch. This is your second cast-on stitch.

4 / Transfer the new stitch to the left-hand needle.

5 / To make your third cast-on stitch, insert your right-hand needle between the two stitches on the left-hand needle. Then wind your yarn around the needle tip, as in step 2.

6 / Use the tip of your needle to pull a loop of yarn through the gap between the stitches and transfer this new stitch to your left-hand needle.

Repeat steps 5 and 6 until you have the number of cast-on stitches that the pattern requires.

Knitting

1 / Insert your right-hand needle, from left to right, into the front of the first stitch to be knitted.

2 / Wind your yarn around the tip of your needle, from left to right.

3 / Use the tip of your needle to draw a loop of yarn through the original stitch. This is your new stitch.

4 / Pull the original stitch off the left-hand needle by gently pulling your right-hand needle further to the right.

Repeat these steps until you have knitted all the stitches on the left-hand needle. To work the next row, put the needle with all the stitches into your left hand, and repeat.

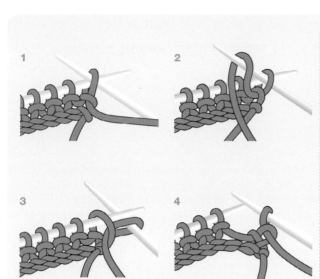

Purling

A purl stitch is like working a knit stitch in reverse.

1 / Making sure your yarn is at the front of your work, insert your right-hand needle from right to left into the front of the first stitch on your left-hand needle.

2 / Wind your yarn around the tip of your needle, from top to bottom.

3 / Use the tip of your needle to pull a loop of yarn through the original stitch. This is your new stitch.

4 / Pull the original stitch off the left-hand needle by gently pulling your right-hand needle further to the right.

Repeat these steps until you have purled all the stitches on the left-hand needle. To work the next row, put the needle with all the stitches into your left hand and repeat.

Binding off knitwise

1 / First, knit two stitches in the normal way. Using the tip of your left-hand needle, lift the first stitch you have knitted over the second knitted stitch.

2 / Knit the next stitch so you have two stitches on your needle again, and repeat the process outlined in step 1.

Continue until you have just one stitch left. Cut the yarn, leaving a fairly long tail that can be used for sewing your item together, and pull it through the last stitch.

Binding off purlwise

This is just like binding off knitwise, but you purl instead of knit the stitches.

1 / First, purl two stitches in the normal way. Using the tip of your left-hand needle, lift the first stitch you have purled over the second purled stitch.

2 / Purl the next stitch so you have two stitches on your needle again, and repeat the process outlined in step 1.

Combining knit and purl stitches

When you knit every row, the knitted fabric you produce is called garter stitch. When you work alternate rows of knit and purl stitches, the knitted fabric you produce is called stockinette stitch (abbreviated in knitting patterns to "st st"). These two combinations are the main stitches used in all of the projects in this book.

Shaping up nicely

Most of the projects in this book involve a fair amount of shaping. Shaping in knitting involves both decreasing and increasing the amount of stitches on your needle and there is more than one way of doing this.

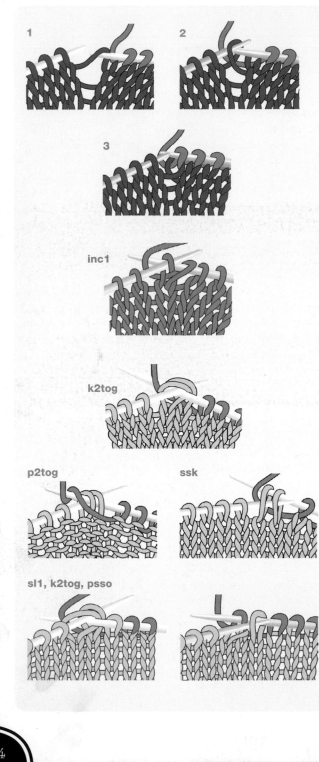

Increasing m1

The main way to increase the number of stitches on your needle is to make an additional stitch between two stitches.

1 / With the tip of your right-hand needle, pick up the horizontal loop between the stitch you have just knitted and the following stitch.

2 / Transfer the loop onto your left-hand needle by inserting the needle into the front of the loop. Then knit into the back of the loop in the normal way.

3 / Your new stitch is now on your right-hand needle.

Increasing inc1

This is an alternative method of increasing the number of stitches.

Begin by knitting your stitch in the normal way, but rather than slipping the original stitch off the needle, knit again into the back of the original stitch and then slip the original stitch off the needle.

Decreasing k2tog

This is the simplest way of decreasing. Put your needle through two stitches instead of just one, then knit them in the normal way.

Decreasing p2tog

This is just like knitting two stitches together, only you purl the stitches instead of knitting them.

Decreasing ssk

This forms a mirror image to the right-sloping stitch formed by knitting two stitches together.

First slip one stitch kwise, then the next kwise, from your left-hand needle to the right-hand needle. Insert the tip of your left-hand needle from left to right through the front of the two slipped stitches, then knit in the normal way.

Decreasing sl1, k2tog, psso

Occasionally you will need to decrease two stitches at a time.

To do this, first slip one stitch from your left- to your right-hand needle pwise. Then knit two stitches together, as outlined above. Finally, pass the slipped stitch over the stitch you have just made by knitting the two stitches together.

Get it together

One of the most crucial parts of knitting is sewing your project pieces together. This is always done with the yarn you have used to knit the pieces and a yarn needle. To achieve the best results, take a bit of time to study the different methods

Mattress stitch

This is used to seam vertical edges such as the side seams of bodies and garments. A slight variation of the standard mattress stitch can also be used to join two horizontal edges such as the lower edges of the character's bodies.

Vertical edges

With the two vertical edges together, take your yarn under the running stitch between the first two stitches on one side, then under the running stitch between the first two stitches on the other side. Continue threading your yarn up the seam in this way, pulling the yarn up quite firmly every few stitches.

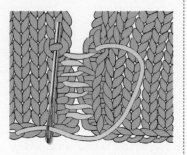

Horizontal edges

With the two horizontal edges together, take your yarn around the two "legs" of the outermost row of stitches on one piece of knitting and then under the two corresponding "legs" of the second piece of knitting. Continue in this way, pulling the yarn up quite firmly every few stitches.

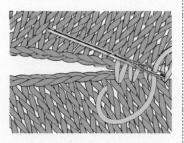

A jolly good dunk

Sometimes when you have stitched an item together, the shape is not exactly as you want. If this is the case, it is helpful to soak the item with cold or lukewarm water, squeeze out the excess water, reshape the item, and then leave it to dry.

Overcast stitch or oversewing

This is used for seaming curved edges or for sewing very small items together. For some projects, you will use a combination of oversewing and mattress stitch. Usually overcast stitch is used on the reverse side of your work (with the right sides of your knitting together), but sometimes it is used on the outside of your work.

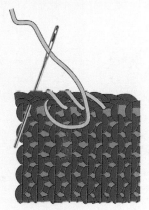

To oversew a seam, take your yarn from the front over the edges of your seam and back through the front, a little further along.

Picking up stitches along an edge

Although this is not strictly a joining technique, sometimes you will need to pick up stitches along either a vertical or a horizontal edge of your knitting, in order to knit another part of the project.

With the right side of your work facing you, insert your needle into the first stitch at the point where you want to create a new stitch. Wind the yarn around the tip of your needle and pull the new loop through, as if knitting a normal stitch. Continue until you have the required number of stitches. Remember, if you are picking up stitches along a vertical edge, you may have more stitches along the edge than you need to pick up. If this is the case, you will need to miss picking up a stitch occasionally.

Vertical

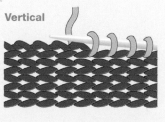

Horizontal

Finishing touches

To add the final flourish to your knitted items, you will need to know a few basic embroidery stitches and also how to work a simple crochet chain. This section tells you all the techniques you need to know and also gives you a few tips on finishing touches that will ensure your work looks professional.

French knot

Chain stitch

Straight stitch

Star stitch

French knot

This is used for the center of the dolls' and creatures' eyes and for some of the decoration on the large Christmas stocking (see page 20).

Bring your yarn out at your starting point, between the strands of yarn, keeping your needle fairly close to the surface of your knitting. Wind the yarn twice around your needle, keeping the yarn fairly taut. Take the point of your needle back down into your knitting, next to your starting point, between strands of yarn. Take your needle out at the starting point for the next stitch or in an inconspicuous area where you can secure and trim the yarn. Pull your yarn through your work so that the knot slides off the needle and onto your knitting.

Chain stitch

This is used for eyes, some of the dolls' hair and features, and for some of the decorations on the large Christmas stocking and wreath (see page 62). You can work chain stitch in rows, curved lines, or circles.

Bring your yarn out at your starting point. Take your needle back into your knitting, next to your starting point, leaving a small loop of yarn. Bring your needle back up through your knitting a stitch width along and catch the yarn loop. Pull your yarn up quite firmly. Repeat this process until the stitching is the required length.

Straight stitch

This is used for some of the dolls' and creatures' mouths and eyelashes, and for some of the decoration on the large Christmas stocking.

Simply take your yarn out at your starting point and back down into your knitting where you want the stitch to end. Bring your needle back out at the point where you want to make the next stitch.

Star stitch

This is used for decorating the stockings. Draw the shape on your knitting using a watersoluble pen before working this stitch.

Bring your yarn out at your starting point in the center of the star. Take your needle down into your knitting at the end of the first point of the star and back out again at the end of the second point of the star. Now take your yarn from the second point of the star and back down into the center. Continue in this way until you have worked all eight points of the star.

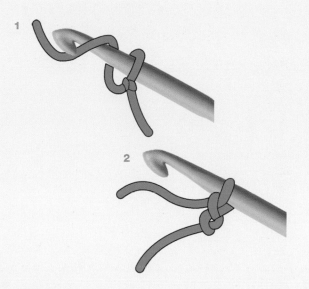

Crochet chains

These are used for some of the dolls' hair, some parts of the dolls' clothes, the cord for St. Nicholas's sack (see page 57), and the hanging loops.

1 / Form a slip knot on your crochet hook, as if you were starting to cast on some knitting. Then wind the yarn around the back of your hook and then to the front, catching the yarn in the slot of the hook.

2 / Use the hook to pull a loop of yarn through the slip stitch to form the second stitch. Continue in this way, pulling the stitches up fairly tightly, until your crochet chain is the required length.

Neat and tidy

To make your work look neat and tidy, it helps to know a few useful tips for concealing and weaving in your yarn ends or "tails" once you have finished sewing your items together. It is also useful to know how to conceal the beginning and end of your work when you are embroidering features or embellishments.

Weaving in ends

You can conceal the yarn ends or "tails" on stuffed items within the item itself. Use your needle to take the yarn end into the item and out again. Squash the item slightly, pull the yarn taut, and trim the yarn close to your knitting.

With items such as the dolls' clothes and the Christmas stockings, weave in the yarn tails by working a few running stitches backward and forward along the seam allowance. It helps to work the running stitches between the strands as this helps them stay put—so you may want to use your embroidery rather than a tapestry or darning needle to do this.

Concealing yarns when embroidering

To begin embroidering features on the dolls and creatures, tie a double knot in the end of your yarn. Take your needle between stitches at the back of your work (or a nearby inconspicuous area) and out to your starting point.

Pull the yarn firmly, so that the knot disappears into the inside of your work. When you have finished the embroidery, take your yarn back out to an inconspicuous area. Pull the yarn fairly firmly and work a couple of tiny stitches, one over the other, around the running thread between the knitted stitches. (The running threads will be slightly sunken so the stitches will be virtually invisible.) Conceal the remaining yarn tail in the same way that you would normally conceal yarn tails on stuffed items (see above).

When you are working embroidery on a flat item such as the Christmas stockings, you can simply tie a knot in your yarn at both the beginning and end of your work, and trim them closely.

'TWAS the night before Christmas, when all through the house Not a creature was stirring, not even a mouse; The stockings were hung by the chimney with care, In hopes that ST. NICHOLAS soon would be there;

Christmas stockings

Christmas stockings originated from long-ago tales of St. Nicholas. When he saw a family of poor girls hanging their stockings to dry by the fire, he dropped bags of coins down the chimney to land in each stocking. This pair of traditional wooly stockings is embellished with an embroidered snowflake.

Large stocking

Side 1
Make 1
• Cast on 44 sts in bright red.
• 1st row: K1, inc1, K to last 3 sts, inc1, K to end. [46 sts]
• Next and every ws row: P.
• Next rs row: K2, m1, K to last 2 sts, m1, K2. [48 sts]
• Next rs row: K2, m1, K to last 2 sts, m1, K2. [50 sts]
• Next rs row: K2, m1, K to end. [51 sts]
• Next rs row: K2, m1, K to end. [52 sts]
• Next rs row: K2, m1, K to end. [53 sts]
• Next row: P.
• Work 8 rows in st st beg with a K row.
• Next row: K2, k2tog, K to end. [52 sts]
• Next row: P.
• Rep last 2 rows four times more. [48 sts]
• Next row: Bind off 23 sts, K to end. [25 sts]
• Next row: P.
• Next row: K2, k2tog, K to end. [24 sts]
• Work 5 rows in st st beg with a P row.

• Next row: K2, m1, K to last 2 sts, m1, K2. [26 sts]
• Work 15 rows in st st beg with a P row.
• Rep last 16 rows three times more. [32 sts]
• Next row: K2, m1, K to last 2 sts, m1, K2. [34 sts]
• Work 3 rows in st st beg with a P row.
• Break bright red yarn and join lime green yarn.
• K 2 rows.
• Join cream yarn, but don't break lime green yarn.
• Using cream yarn, work 4 rows in st st beg with a K row.
• Using lime green yarn, K 2 rows.
• Using cream yarn, work 4 rows in st st beg with a K row.
• Rep last 6 rows once more.
• Using lime green yarn, K 4 rows.
• Bind off loosely.

Side 2
Make 1
• Cast on 44 sts in bright red.

- 1st row: K3, inc1, K to last st, inc1, K1. [46 sts]
- Next and every ws row: P.
- Next rs row: K2, m1, K to last 2 sts, m1, K2. [48 sts]
- Next rs row: K2, m1, K to last 2 sts, m1, K2. [50 sts]
- Next rs row: K to last 2 sts, m1, K2. [51 sts]
- Next rs row: K to last 2 sts, m1, K2. [52 sts]
- Next rs row: K to last 2 sts, m1, K2. [53 sts]
- Next row: P.
- Work 8 rows in st st beg with a K row.
- Next row: K to last 4 sts, ssk, K2. [52 sts]
- Next row: P.
- Rep last 2 rows four times more. [48 sts]
- Next row: K.
- Next row: Bind off 23 sts pwise, P to end. [25 sts]
- Next row: K to last 4 sts, ssk, K2. [24 sts]
- Work 5 rows in st st beg with a P row.
- Next row: K2, m1, K to last 2 sts, m1, K2. [26 sts]
- Work 15 rows in st st beg with a P row.
- Rep last 16 rows three times more. [32 sts]
- Next row: K2, m1, K to last 2 sts, m1, K2. [34 sts]
- Work 3 rows in st st beg with a P row.
- Break bright red yarn and join lime green yarn.
- K 2 rows.
- Join cream yarn, but don't break lime green yarn.
- Using cream yarn, work 4 rows in st st beg with a K row.
- Using lime green yarn, K 2 rows.
- Using cream yarn, work 4 rows in st st beg with a K row.
- Rep last 6 rows once more.
- Using lime green yarn, K 4 rows.
- Bind off loosely.

To finish

Decorate the stocking using the photograph as a guide. Use a watersoluble marking pen to draw the outline of a snowflake on one side of your stocking. Using cream yarn, embroider the main lines of the snowflake in chain stitch, the central star in star stitch, and the "branches" in straight stitches. The dots between the branches are French knots.

Use the watersoluble pen to mark the heel and toe sections of the stocking on both sides. Embroider these lines in chain stitch, using lime green yarn.

To make up, place the sides of the two stocking pieces together and sew the seams using mattress stitch. For the stocking loop, use the crochet hook and bright red yarn to make a 5-in (13-cm) crochet chain. Sew the loop to the seam at the back of the stocking.

Mini stocking

Side 1

Make 1
- Cast on 14 sts in bright red.
- 1st row: K1, inc1, K to last 3 sts, inc1, K to end. [16 sts]
- Next and every ws row: P.
- Next rs row: K2, m1, K to last 2 sts, m1, K2. [18 sts]
- Next rs row: K2, m1, K to last 2 sts, m1, K2. [20 sts]
- Next rs row: K to last 2 sts, m1, K2. [21 sts]
- Next rs row: K to last 4 sts, k2tog, K2. [20 sts]
- Next rs row: K to last 4 sts, k2tog, K2. [19 sts]
- Next rs row: K to last 4 sts, k2tog, K2. [18 sts]
- Next row: Bind off 8 sts pwise, P to end. [10 sts]
- Work 4 rows in st st beg with a K row.
- * Next row: K1, m1, K to last st, m1, K1. [12 sts]
- Work 5 rows in st st beg with a P row.

- Next row: K1, m1, K to last st, m1, K1. [14 sts]
- Work 5 rows in st st beg with a P row.
- Next row: K1, m1, K to last st, m1, K1. [16 sts]
- Next row: P.
- Break bright red yarn and join lime green yarn.
- K 2 rows.
- Join cream yarn, but don't break lime green yarn.
- Using cream yarn, work 2 rows in st st beg with a K row.
- Rep last 4 rows once more.
- Using lime green yarn, K 2 rows.
- Bind off loosely.

Side 2

Make 1
- Cast on 14 sts in bright red.
- 1st row: K3, inc1, K to last st, inc1, K1. [16 sts]
- Next and every ws row: P
- Next rs row: K2, m1, K to last 2 sts, m1, K2. [18 sts]
- Next rs row: K2, m1, K to last 2 sts, m1, K2. [20 sts]
- Next rs row: K2, m1, K to end. [21 sts]
- Next rs row: K2, k2tog, K to end. [20 sts]
- Next rs row: K2, k2tog, K to end. [19 sts]
- Next rs row: K2, k2tog, K to end. [18 sts]
- Next rs row: Bind off 8 sts, K to end. [10 sts]
- Work 3 rows in st st beg with a P row.
- Continue as side 1 from * to end.

To finish

Using cream yarn, embroider a star in star stitch on the front of one side of the stocking using the photograph as a guide.

For the stocking loop, use the crochet hook and bright red yarn to make a 2-in (5-cm) crochet chain.

Join the stocking pieces and attach the loop as for the large stocking.

The children were nestled
all snug in their beds,
While visions of sugar-plums
danced in their heads.

Baby

It's his very first Christmas Eve—and what a lively night it's turned out to be. This little baby is dressed in a turquoise all-in-one suit that's knitted as part of the doll itself. We've made a baby boy—but if you want to knit a baby girl, choose a pretty pastel pink and, if you like, add a little more hair.

YOU WILL NEED

FOR THE DOLL AND CLOTHES

* ⅛ oz/5 g (16 yds/15 m) turquoise DK yarn
* ⅛ oz/5 g (16 yds/15 m) beige DK yarn
* Very small amounts of black, cream, and red DK yarn
* Small amount of dark brown DK yarn
* ⅜ oz/10 g polyester filling
* Two tiny purple star-shaped buttons
* **Size 2/3 (3 mm) knitting needles**
* **Size D-3 (3.25 mm) or similar crochet hook**

Body & head

The body and head are knitted as one piece, from the base of the body to the top of the head.

Front

Make 1

* Cast on 8 sts in turquoise.
* Work 2 rows in st st beg with a K row.
* Next row: K2, m1, K4, m1, K2. [10 sts]
* Next row: P.
* Next row: K2, m1, K6, m1, K2. [12 sts]
* Work 5 rows in st st beg with a P row.
* Next row: K2, k2tog, K4, ssk, K2. [10 sts]
* Next row: p2tog, P6, p2tog. [8 sts]
* Next row: K2, k2tog, ssk, K2. [6 sts]
* Next row: K.
* Break yarn and join beige yarn.
* Work 2 rows in st st beg with a K row.
* Next row: (K1, m1) twice, K2, (m1, K1) twice. [10 sts]
* Next row: P.
* Next row: K2, m1, K1, m1, K4, m1, K1, m1, K2. [14 sts]
* Next row: P.
* Next row: K2, m1, K10, m1, K2. [16 sts]
* Next row: P.*

• Next row: K7, K into f and b of next 2 sts, turn, P4, turn back and K to end. [18 sts]
• Next row: P7, (p2tog) twice, P7. [16 sts]
• Work 4 rows in st st beg with a K row.
• Next row: K2, (k2tog) twice, K4, (ssk) twice, K2. [12 sts]
• Next row: (p2tog) twice, P4, (p2tog) twice. [8 sts]
• Next row: (k2tog) twice, (ssk) twice. [4 sts]
• Bind off pwise.

Back
Make 1
• Work as for front as far as ^.
• Work 6 rows in st st beg with a K row.
• Next row: K2, (k2tog) twice, K4, (ssk) twice, K2. [12 sts]
• Next row: (p2tog) twice, P4, (p2tog) twice. [8 sts]
• Next row: (k2tog) twice, (ssk) twice. [4 sts]
• Bind off pwise.

Legs & feet
The legs and feet are knitted as one piece, from the bottom of the foot to the top of the thigh.
Make 2
• Cast on 20 sts in turquoise.
• Work 4 rows in st st beg with a K row.
• Next row: K5, Bind off 10 sts, K to end. [10 sts]
• Work 5 rows in st st beg with a P row.
• Bind off.

Arms
The arms are knitted from the top of the arm to the tip of the hand.
Make 2
• Cast on 8 sts in turquoise.
• Work 9 rows in st st beg with a K row.
• Next row: K.
• Break yarn and join beige yarn.
• Work 2 rows in st st beg with a K row.
• Next row: k2tog, K4, k2tog. [6 sts]
• Next row: p2tog, P2, p2tog. [4 sts]
• Bind off.

Making up
Place the two body and head pieces right sides together. Oversew around the sides and top of the head. Turn the piece the right sides out and seam the sides of the body using mattress stitch, leaving the lower edge open for stuffing. Stuff and then sew the gap closed.

Fold the leg pieces lengthwise so the right side is on the inside. Oversew the lower, back, and top seams of the feet. Turn the pieces the right way out and sew the back seams using mattress stitch. Stuff the legs and feet.

Fold the arm pieces lengthwise so the right side is on the inside. Oversew around the hand. Turn the pieces the right way out and sew the arm seams using mattress stitch. The arms do not need to be stuffed.

Join the arms to the top of the main body and the legs to the lower part of the body.

Sew the purple star-shaped buttons to the front of the baby's suit.

Using black yarn, embroider two French knots for the eyes. Using cream yarn, work a ring of chain stitch around each French knot. Separate a short length of red yarn lengthwise, so that you have two thinner lengths of yarn. Use one length to work two straight stitches, one on top of the other, for the mouth. Use a red crayon to color the cheeks.

For the hair, use the crochet hook and dark brown yarn to make a 5-in (13-cm) crochet chain. Arrange it into three loops and fasten it to the top of the head, using the photograph as a guide.

Daughter

She may look as if butter wouldn't melt in her mouth, but this little girl knows just what she wants—and this Christmas, it looks like all her wishes will come true. She's knitted here in a vivid pink nightdress, because almost all little girls love pink. But the nightdress would work just as well in pastel tones, so the choice is entirely yours.

Doll

Body & head

The body and head are knitted as one piece, from the base of the body to the top of the head.

Front

Make 1

• Cast on 10 sts in flesh.
• Work 2 rows in st st beg with a K row.
• Next row: K2, m1, K6, m1, K2. [12 sts]
• Next row: P.
• Next row: K2, m1, K8, m1, K2. [14 sts]
• Work 7 rows in st st beg with a P row.
• Next row: K2, k2tog, K6, ssk, K2. [12 sts]
• Next row: p2tog, P8, p2tog. [10 sts]
• Next row: K2, k2tog, K2, ssk, K2. [8 sts]
• Next row: p2tog, P4, p2tog. [6 sts]
• Next row: (K1, m1) twice, K2, (m1, K1) twice. [10 sts]
• Next row: P.
• Next row: K2, m1, K1, m1, K4, m1, K1, m1, K2. [14 sts]
• Next row: P.
• Next row: K2, m1, K10, m1, K2.* [16 sts]
• Work 3 rows in st st beg with a P row.
• Next row: K7, K into f and b of next 2 sts, turn, P4, turn back and K to end. [18 sts]

- Next row: P7, (p2tog) twice, P7. [16 sts]
- Work 4 rows in st st beg with a K row.
- Next row: K2, (k2tog) twice, K4, (ssk) twice, K2. [12 sts]
- Next row: (p2tog) twice, P4, (p2tog) twice. [8 sts]
- Next row: (k2tog) twice, (ssk) twice. [4 sts]
- Bind off pwise.

Back
Make 1
- Work as for front as far as *.
- Next row: P.
- Break yarn and join rust yarn for hair.
- Work 8 rows in st st beg with a K row.
- Next row: K2, (k2tog) twice, K4, (ssk) twice, K2. [12 sts]
- Next row: (p2tog) twice, P4, (p2tog) twice. [8 sts]
- Next row: (k2tog) twice, (ssk) twice. [4 sts]
- Bind off pwise.

Legs & feet
The legs and feet are knitted as one piece, from the bottom of the foot to the top of the thigh.
Make 2
- Cast on 22 sts in flesh.
- Work 4 rows in st st beg with a K row.
- Next row: K6, bind off 10 sts, K to end. [12 sts]
- Work 11 rows in st st beg with a P row.
- Bind off.

Arms
The arms are knitted from the top of the arm to the tip of the hand.
Make 2
- Cast on 9 sts in flesh.
- Work 16 rows in st st beg with a K row.
- Next row: K4, K into f and b of next st, turn, P2, turn again and K to end. [10 sts]
- Next row: P4, p2tog, P4. [9 sts]
- Next row: K.
- Next row: p2tog, P5, p2tog. [7 sts]
- Next row: k2tog, K3, ssk. [5 sts]
- Bind off pwise.

Making up
Place the two body and head pieces right sides together. Oversew around the sides and top of the head. Turn the piece the right sides out and seam the sides of the body using mattress stitch, leaving the lower edge open for stuffing. Stuff and then sew the gap closed.

Fold the leg pieces lengthwise so the right side is on the inside. Oversew the lower, back, and top seams of the feet. Turn the pieces the right way out and sew the back seams using mattress stitch. Stuff the legs and feet.

Fold the arm pieces lengthwise so the right side is on the inside. Oversew around the hand. Turn the pieces the right way out and sew the arm seams using mattress stitch. The arms do not need to be stuffed.

Join the arms to the top of the main body and the legs to the lower part of the body.

Using black yarn, embroider two French knots for the eyes. Using cream yarn, work two rings of chain stitch around each French knot. Separate a length of black yarn into separate strands and use one of these to work three straight stitches above each eye for the eyelashes. Separate a short length of red yarn lengthwise, so that you have two thinner lengths of yarn. Use one length to work two straight stitches, one on top of the other, for the mouth. Use a red crayon to color the cheeks.

For the hair, using rust yarn, embroider a few rows of chain stitch across the head from one side to the other. For the braids, thread two 12-in (30-cm) lengths of the same yarn through the head, at the lower edge of the chain stitch, so that you have four shorter lengths. Using two single strands and one double strand, make a 2-in (5-cm) braid and knot the ends. Work the second braid in the same way.

Nightdress

Dress
Make 2
- Cast on 22 sts in bright pink.
- K 2 rows.
- Work 5 rows st st beg with a P row.
- Next row: K2, k2tog, K14, ssk, K2. [20 sts]
- Work 5 rows in st st beg with a P row.
- Next row: K2, k2tog, K12, ssk, K2. [18 sts]
- Work 5 rows in st st beg with a P row.
- Next row: k2tog, (P1, K1) 7 times, p2tog. [16 sts]
- Next row: (P1, K1) 8 times.
- Next row: (K1, P1) 8 times.
- Rep last 2 rows twice more.
- Next row: (P1, K1) 8 times.
- Bind off knitwise.

With the right sides of the nightdress together, oversew ¼ in/5 mm at each side of the neck edge to form the shoulder seams.

Sleeves
Make 2
- With the right side of your work facing you, pick up and knit 7 sts from just below the seed stitch yoke to the shoulder seam, then another 7 sts from the shoulder seam to the end of the yoke on the other side. [14 sts]
- Work 7 rows in st st beg with a P row.
- K 2 rows.
- Bind off.

Making up
Join the side and sleeve seams using mattress stitch. Sew the small heart-shaped button onto the front of the yoke using the pink yarn.

And Mamma in her 'kerchief,
and I in my cap,
Had just settled down
for a long
winter's
nap,

When out on the lawn there arose such a clatter,
I sprang from the bed to see what was the matter.
Away to the window I flew like a flash,
Tore open the *shutters* and
threw up the sash.

Father

He is one of those fathers whose home is his castle, so it's no wonder he leapt out of bed to investigate the clatter on the lawn. With his matching nightcap and socks, not to mention the traditional striped nightshirt, the father of the household has an eye for a snazzy outfit. Knit him in the subdued colors we've chosen here, or choose a riot of clashing colors to stamp him with your own personality.

Doll

Body & head

The body and head are knitted as one piece, from the base of the body to the top of the head.

Front

Make 1

* Cast on 14 sts in beige.
* Work 2 rows in st st beg with a K row.
* Next row: K2, m1, K10, m1, K2. [16 sts]
* Next row: P.
* Next row: K2, m1, K12, m1, K2. [18 sts]
* Work 15 rows in st st beg with a P row.
* Next row: K2, k2tog, K10, ssk, K2. [16 sts]
* Next row: p2tog, P12, p2tog. [14 sts]
* Next row: K2, k2tog, K6, ssk, K2. [12 sts]
* Next row: p2tog, P8, p2tog. [10 sts]
* Next row: K2, k2tog, K2, ssk, K2. [8 sts]
* Next row: P.
* Next row: K2, m1, K1, m1, K2, m1, K1, m1, K2. [12 sts]
* Next row: P.
* Next row: K2, (m1, K1) twice, m1, K4, (m1, K1) twice, m1, K2. [18 sts]

- Next row: P.
- Next row: K2, m1, K14, m1, K2. [20 sts]
- Work 3 rows in st st beg with a P row.*
- Next row: K9, K into f and b of next 2 sts, turn, P4, turn back and K to end. [22 sts]
- Next row: P9, (p2tog) twice, P9. [20 sts]
- Work 4 rows in st st beg with a K row.
- Next row: K2, (k2tog) 3 times, K4, (ssk) 3 times, K2. [14 sts]
- Next row: (p2tog) twice, P6, (p2tog) twice. [10 sts]
- Next row: (k2tog) twice, K2, (ssk) twice. [6 sts]
- Bind off pwise.

Back
Make 1
- Work as for front as far as *.
- Break yarn and join dark gray yarn for hair.
- Work 6 rows in st st beg with a K row.

- Next row: K2, (k2tog) 3 times, K4, (ssk) 3 times, K2. [14 sts]
- Next row: (p2tog) twice, P6, (p2tog) twice. [10 sts]
- Next row: (k2tog) twice, K2, (ssk) twice. [6 sts]
- Bind off pwise.

Legs & socks
The legs and socks are knitted as one piece, from the bottom of the foot to the top of the thigh.
Make 2
- Cast on 26 sts in teal.
- Work 6 rows in st st beg with a K row.
- Next row: K6, bind off 14 sts, K to end. [12 sts]
- Work 6 rows in st st beg with a P row.
- Next row: K.
- Break yarn and join beige yarn.
- Work 18 rows in st st beg with a K row.
- Bind off.

Arms
The arms are knitted from the top of the arm to the tip of the hand.
Make 2
- Cast on 9 sts in beige.
- Work 20 rows in st st beg with a K row.
- Next row: K4, K into f and b of next st, turn, P2, turn again and K to end. [10 sts]
- Next row: P4, p2tog, P4. [9 sts]
- Work 2 rows in st st beg with a K row.
- Next row: K1, k2tog, K3, ssk, K1. [7 sts]
- Next row: p2tog, P3, p2tog. [5 sts]
- Bind off.

Making up
Place the two body and head pieces right sides together. Oversew around the sides and top of the head. Turn the piece the right sides out and seam the sides of the body using mattress stitch, leaving the lower edge open for stuffing. Stuff and then sew the gap closed.

Fold the leg pieces lengthwise so the right side is on the inside. Oversew the lower, back, and top seams of the socks. Turn the pieces the right way out and sew the back seams using mattress stitch. Stuff the legs and socks.

Fold the arm pieces lengthwise so the right side is on the inside. Oversew around the hand. Turn the pieces the right way out and sew the arm seams using mattress stitch. The arms do not need to be stuffed.

Join the arms to the top of the main body and the legs to the lower part of the body.

Using black yarn, embroider two French knots for the eyes. Using cream yarn, work a ring of chain stitch around each French knot, then work a short curved row of chain stitch around the bottom part of the eye to give the father the appearance of looking upward. Separate a short length of red yarn lengthwise, so that you have two thinner lengths of yarn. Use one length to work two straight stitches, one on top of the other, for the mouth. Use a red crayon to color the cheeks.

For the hair, embroider a few rows of chain stitch in dark gray yarn, from one side of the head, over the forehead, and down to the other side of the head, using the photograph as a guide.

Nightshirt

Back
Make 1
- Cast on 18 sts in lime green.
- 1st row: K.
- Next row: K2, m1, K to last 2 sts, m1, K2. [20 sts]
- Next row: K2, P to last 2 sts, K2.
- Rep last 2 rows twice more. [24 sts]
- Leave lime green yarn at side and join cream yarn.
- Next row: K.

- Next row: K2, P to last 2 sts, K2.
- Leave cream yarn at side and pick up lime green yarn.
- Work 4 rows in st st beg with a K row.
- Leave lime green yarn at side and pick up cream yarn.
- Work 2 rows in st st beg with a K row.
- Leave cream yarn at side and pick up lime green yarn.
- Work 2 rows st st.
- Next row: K2, k2tog, K to last 4 sts, ssk, K2. [22 sts]
- Next row: P.
- Leave lime green yarn at side and pick up cream yarn.
- Work 2 rows in st st beg with a K row.
- Leave cream yarn at side and pick up lime green yarn.
- Work 2 rows in st st.
- Place a thread marker at each end of last row.
- Next row: K2, k2tog, K to last 4 sts, ssk, K2. [20 sts]
- Next row: P.
- Leave lime green yarn at side and pick up cream yarn.*
- Work 2 rows in st st beg with a K row.
- Break cream yarn and pick up lime green yarn.
- Work 4 rows in st st beg with a K row.
- Next row: Bind off 4 sts, K to end. [16 sts]
- Rep last row once more. [12 sts]
- K 2 rows.
- Bind off.

Front
Make 1
- Work as for back as far as *.
- Next row: K10, turn and cont work on these 10 sts only, leaving rem 10 sts on needle.
- Next row: K2, P to end.
- Break cream yarn and pick up lime green yarn.
- Next row: K.
- Next row: K2, P to end.
- Rep last 2 rows once more.
- Next row: Bind off 4 sts, K to end. [6 sts]

- K 3 rows.
- Bind off.
- With rs of your work facing you, join cream yarn to neck edge of rem 10 sts.
- Next row: K.
- Next row: P to last 2 sts, K2.
- Break cream yarn and pick up lime green yarn.
- Next row: K.
- Next row: P to last 2 sts, K2.
- Rep last 2 rows once more.
- Next row: K.
- Next row: Bind off 4 sts, K to end. [6 sts]
- K 2 rows.
- Bind off.

With right sides of the nightshirt together, oversew shoulder and collar seams.

Sleeves
Make 2
- With the right side of your work facing you, using lime green yarn, pick up and knit 8 sts from thread marker on front to shoulder seam, then pick up and knit another 8 sts from shoulder seam to thread marker on back. [16 sts]
- Work 3 rows in st st beg with a P row.
- Leave lime green yarn at side and pick up cream yarn.
- Work 2 rows in st st beg with a K row.
- Leave cream yarn at side and pick up lime green yarn.
- Work 4 rows in st st beg with a K row.
- Rep last 6 rows once more.
- Bind off.

Making up
Join the side and sleeve seams with lime green yarn using mattress stitch. Knot together the cream threads at the bottom of the V neck on the front of the nightshirt. Run both ends of yarn across one side of the nightshirt and secure in the seam.

Hat
Make 1
- Cast on 32 sts in teal.
- K 2 rows.
- Work 10 rows in st st beg with a K row.
- Next row: K7, ssk, K14, k2tog, K7. [30 sts]
- Next and every ws row: P.
- Next rs row: K6, ssk, K14, k2tog, K6. [28 sts]
- Next rs row: K6, ssk, K12, k2tog, K6. [26 sts]
- Next rs row: K5, ssk, K12, k2tog, K5. [24 sts]
- Next rs row: K5, ssk, K10, k2tog, K5. [22 sts]
- Next rs row: K4, ssk, K10, k2tog, K4. [20 sts]
- Next rs row: K4, ssk, K8, k2tog, K4. [18 sts]
- Next rs row: K3, ssk, K8, k2tog, K3. [16 sts]
- Next rs row: K3, ssk, K6, k2tog, K3. [14 sts]
- Next rs row: K2, ssk, K6, k2tog, K2. [12 sts]
- Next rs row: K2, ssk, K4, k2tog, K2. [10 sts]
- Next rs row: K1, ssk, K4, k2tog, K1. [8 sts]
- Next rs row: K1, ssk, K2, k2tog, K1. [6 sts]
- Next rs row: ssk, K2, k2tog. [4 sts]
- Next rs row: ssk, k2tog. [2 sts]
- Next rs row: k2tog. [1 st]
- Break yarn and pull it through rem st.

To make up, join the back seam using mattress stitch.

Mother

Like so many mothers, this one runs a meticulous home, so it must have been a shock to hear St. Nicholas tumble down the chimney into the fireplace and to see all the ash on the hearth rug. Her pale pink nightdress is a nod to her feminine charms, while her purple kerchief and fur-trimmed slippers are a more practical nod to the chilly December weather.

YOU WILL NEED

FOR THE DOLL

* ½ oz/15 g (44 yds/40 m) flesh DK yarn
* Small amount of rust DK yarn
* Very small amounts of black, cream, and red DK yarn
* ¾ oz/20 g polyester filling

FOR THE CLOTHES

* ⅜ oz/10 g (33 yds/30 m) pale pink DK yarn
* Small amounts of purple and cerise DK yarn
* Small amount of cream mohair yarn
* A pink star-shaped button

Size 2/3 (3 mm) knitting needles

Size D-3 (3.25 mm) or similar crochet hook

Doll

Body & head

The body and head are knitted as one piece, from the base of the body to the top of the head.

Front

Make 1

* Cast on 14 sts in flesh.
* Work 2 rows in st st beg with a K row.
* Next row: K2, m1, K10, m1, K2. [16 sts]
* Next row: P.
* Next row: K2, m1, K12, m1, K2. [18 sts]
* Work 11 rows in st st beg with a P row.
* Next row: K2, k2tog, K10, ssk, K2. [16 sts]
* Next row: p2tog, P12, p2tog. [14 sts]
* Next row: K2, k2tog, K6, ssk, K2. [12 sts]
* Next row: p2tog, P8, p2tog. [10 sts]

- Next row: K2, k2tog, K2, ssk, K2. [8 sts]
- Next row: P.
- Next row: K2, m1, K1, m1, K2, m1, K1, m1, K2. [12 sts]
- Next row: P.
- Next row: K2, m1, (K1, m1) twice, K4, (m1, K1) twice, m1, K2. [18 sts]
- Next row: P.
- Next row: K2, m1, K14, m1, K2.* [20 sts]
- Work 3 rows in st st beg with a P row.
- Next row: K9, K into f and b of next 2 sts, turn, P4, turn back and K to end. [22 sts]
- Next row: P9, (p2tog) twice, P9. [20 sts]
- Work 4 rows in st st beg with a K row.
- Next row: K2, (k2tog) 3 times, K4, (ssk) 3 times, K2. [14 sts]
- Next row: (p2tog) twice, P6, (p2tog) twice. [10 sts]
- Next row: (k2tog) twice, K2, (ssk) twice. [6 sts]
- Bind off pwise.

Back
Make 1
- Work as for front as far as *.
- Next row: P.
- Break yarn and join rust yarn for hair.
- Work 8 rows in st st beg with a P row.
- Next row: K2, (k2tog) 3 times, K4, (ssk) 3 times, K2. [14 sts]
- Next row: (p2tog) twice, P6, (p2tog) twice. [10 sts]
- Next row: (k2tog) twice, K2, (ssk) twice. [6 sts]
- Bind off pwise.

Legs & feet
The legs and feet are knitted as one piece, from the bottom of the foot to the top of the thigh.
Make 2
- Cast on 24 sts in flesh.
- Work 4 rows in st st beg with a K row.
- Next row: K6, bind off 12 sts, K to end. [12 sts]
- Work 23 rows in st st beg with a P row.
- Bind off.

Arms
The arms are knitted from the top of the arm to the tip of the hand.
Make 2
- Cast on 9 sts in flesh.
- Work 20 rows in st st beg with a K row.
- Next row: K4, K into f and b of next st, turn, P2, turn again and K to end. [10 sts]
- Next row: P4, p2tog, P4. [9 sts]
- Work 2 rows in st st beg with a K row.
- Next row: K1, k2tog, K3, ssk, K1. [7 sts]
- Next row: p2tog, P3, p2tog. [5 sts]
- Bind off.

Making up
Place the two body and head pieces right sides together. Oversew around the sides and top of the head. Turn the piece the right sides out and seam the sides of the body using mattress stitch, leaving the lower edge open for stuffing. Stuff and then sew the gap closed.

Fold the leg pieces lengthwise so the right side is on the inside. Oversew the lower, back, and top seams of the feet. Turn the pieces the right way out and sew the back seams using mattress stitch. Stuff the legs and feet.

Fold the arm pieces lengthwise so the right side is on the inside. Oversew around the hand. Turn the pieces the right way out and sew the arm seams using mattress stitch. The arms do not need to be stuffed.

Join the arms to the top of the main body and the legs to the lower part of the body.

Using black yarn, embroider two French knots for the eyes. Using cream yarn, work two rings of chain stitch around each French knot. Separate a length of black yarn into separate strands and use one of these to work three straight stitches above each eye for the eyelashes. Separate a short length of red yarn lengthwise, so that you have two thinner lengths of yarn. Use one length to work two straight stitches, one on top of the other, for the mouth. Use a red crayon to color the cheeks.

For the hair, using rust yarn, embroider a few rows of chain stitch from one side of the head to the other and at the front of the head, curving the rows at the forehead. Use the crochet hook and rust yarn to make two 4-in (10-cm) crochet chains. Arrange the chains in two loops at each side of the head, as shown in the photograph.

Nightdress

Front

Make 1
- Cast on 30 sts in pale pink.
- 1st row: K.
- Next row: P1, (yo, p2tog) to last st, P1. [30 sts]
- K 3 rows.
- Work 7 rows in st st beg with a P row.
- Next row: K2, k2tog, K to last 4 sts, ssk, K2. [28 sts]
- Work 3 rows in st st beg with a P row.
- Rep last 4 rows twice more. [24 sts]
- Next row: K2, (k2tog, K1) 6 times, K2tog, K2. [17 sts]
- Next row: K.*
- Next row: K7, k2tog. [8 sts]
- Turn and cont working on these sts only, leaving rem sts on needle.
- Work 3 rows in st st beg with a P row.
- Next row: K1, k2tog, K2, ssk, K1. [6 sts]
- Next row: P.
- Next row: K1, k2tog, ssk, K1. [4 sts]
- Next row: (p2tog) twice. [2 sts]
- Next row: k2tog, break yarn and pull yarn through rem st, leaving long yarn "tail" (this will be used to make straps for nightdress).
- With rs of your work facing you, join yarn to neck edge of rem 8 sts.
- Work 4 rows in st st beg with a K row.
- Next row: K1, k2tog, K2, ssk, K1. [6 sts]
- Next row: P.
- Next row: K1, k2tog, ssk, K1. [4 sts]

- Next row: (p2tog) twice. [2 sts]
- Next row: k2tog, break yarn and pull yarn through rem st, leaving long yarn "tail" as before, to make straps for nightdress.

Back

Make 1
- Work as for front as far as *.
- Next row: k2tog, K to last 2 sts, ssk. [15 sts]
- Next row: K.
- Bind off.

Making up

Join the side seams using mattress stitch. Using the tail yarn at the center front of the dress, work a couple of stitches to pull the two front sides together slightly, then thread the yarn to one side and secure it in the side seam. Make the nightdress straps by working a 2-in (5-cm) crochet chain from the yarn tail at the top of each side of the front with the crochet hook. Cross the straps at the back and secure each end about ⅜ in (1 cm) in from the side seams. Sew the star button to the front.

Kerchief

The kerchief is made in two parts—the band that goes around the head and a separate bow.

Band

Make 1
- Cast on 35 sts in purple.
- K 4 rows.
- Bind off.

Bow

Make 1
- Cast on 2 sts.
- 1st row: Inc1, K to end. [3 sts]
- Next row: K.
- Next row: K1, m1, K1, m1, K1. [5 sts]
- K 16 rows.

- Next row: k2tog, K1, ssk. [3 sts]
- Next row: K.
- Next row: sl1, k2tog, psso. [1 st]
- Break yarn and pull it through rem st.

Making up

Join the short sides of the hair band. Join the center of the bow to the center of the hair band with several large stitches, pulling them up slightly to gather the center part of the bow.

Slippers

Make 2
- Cast on 26 sts in cerise.
- Work 5 rows in st st beg with a K row.
- Next row: P8, bind off 10 sts, P to end. [16 sts]
- Work 2 rows in st st beg with a K row.
- Break yarn and join cream mohair yarn.
- K 2 rows.
- Bind off.

Making up

Fold one piece widthwise so that the right sides are together. Oversew the short edge, lower seam (cast-on edge), and upper edge. Turn the slipper the right side out and secure loose yarn ends. Complete the second slipper in the same way.

The moon on the breast of the new fallen *snow*,

Gave the luster of mid-day to objects below;

When, what to my wondering eyes should appear,

But a miniature *sleigh*, and eight tiny reindeer,

With a little old driver, so lively and quick,

I knew in a moment it must be St. Nick.

More rapid than eagles his coursers they came,
And he whistled, and shouted, and called them by name;
"Now! Dasher, now! Dancer, now! Prancer, and Vixen,
On! Comet, on! Cupid, on! Donner and Blitzen;
To the top of the porch! To the top of the wall!
Now dash away! Dash away!
Dash away all!"

Reindeer

With their wonky eyes and quirky smiles, these reindeer have more personality than most. Without a shadow of doubt, you'll want to whip yourself up a whole herd. For a bit of authenticity, the reindeer are knitted in a natural alpaca DK yarn, but you could just as easily use a standard double knitting yarn.

YOU WILL NEED

FOR EACH REINDEER

✳ ⅞ oz/25 g (80 yds/73 m) gray/brown DK yarn

✳ Small amounts of dark brown, black, cream, white, and pink, red, or mauve DK yarn

✳ 1 oz/30 g polyester filling

Size 2/3 (3 mm) knitting needles except when instructed to use size 1 (2.25 mm) knitting needles

Dasher

Head & shoulders

The head and shoulders are made first and the body is made by picking up stitches along the edge of the head and shoulders piece and knitting onto it.

Make 1

• Cast on 56 sts in gray/brown.
• 1st row: K14, mark last (14th) st with a contrasting thread, K29, mark last (29th) st with a contrasting thread, K to end.
• Work 9 rows in st st beg with a P row.
• Next row: k2tog, K to last 2 sts, k2tog. [54 sts]
• Next row: p2tog, P to last 2 sts, p2tog. [52 sts]
• Rep last 2 rows once more. [48 sts]
• Next row: Bind off 14 sts, K to end. [34 sts]
• Next row: Bind off 14 sts pwise, P to end. [20 sts]
• Work 2 rows in st st beg with a K row.
• Next row: k2tog, K to last 2 sts, ssk. [18 sts]
• Next row: P.
• Rep last 2 rows twice more. [14 sts]
• Next row: K1, (k2tog, K1) twice, K1, (ssk, K1) twice. [10 sts]
• Next row: p2tog, P to last 2 sts, p2tog. [8 sts]
• Break yarn leaving a long tail and draw yarn through rem sts.

Dancer

Prancer

Vixen

Comet

Cupid

Donner

Blitzen

Body

With the right side of your work facing you, pick up and knit 28 sts along the cast-on edge of the head and shoulders—from one edge to the first marker and then from the second marker to the second edge. (This will leave a loop of knitting that will be stitched together to form the back of the reindeer's neck.)

• Next row: P.
• Next row: K4, (m1, K4) 6 times. [34 sts]
• Work 21 rows in st st beg with a P row.
• Next row: K16, sl2, K to end.
• Next row: P16, sl2, P to end.
• Bind off, taking in the loops formed by the slipped sts on the last two rows as you go.

Front legs

Make 2

• Cast on 12 sts in gray/brown, leaving a long tail for sewing up.
• K 4 rows.
• Work 16 rows in st st beg with a K row.
• Next row: K1, m1, K to last st, m1, K1. [14 sts]
• Work 17 rows in st st beg with a P row.
• Bind off.

Back legs

Make 2

• Cast on 12 sts in gray/brown, leaving a long tail for sewing up.
• K 4 rows.
• Work 16 rows in st st beg with a K row.
• Next row: K1, m1, K to last st, m1, K1. [14 sts]
• Work 3 rows in st st beg with a P row.
• Rep last 4 rows three times more. [20 sts]
• Work 4 rows in st st beg with a K row.
• Bind off.

Ears

Make 2

• Cast on 5 sts in gray/brown.
• K 10 rows.
• Next row: k2tog, K1, ssk. [3 sts]
• Next row: sl1, k2tog, psso. [1 st]
• Break yarn and pull it through rem st.

Tail

Make 1

• Cast on 14 sts in gray/brown.
• Work 4 rows in st st.
• Bind off.

Antlers

Make 2

There are four antler variations. If you are knitting all eight reindeer, we recommend that you knit two pairs of each type.

Version 1
• Cast on 3 sts in dark brown on size 1 (2.25 mm) needles.
• Work 8 rows in st st beg with a K row.

- Next row: Cast on 4 sts, K to end. [7 sts]
- Next row: Cast on 4 sts, P to end. [11 sts]
- Next row: Bind off 4 sts, K to end. [7 sts]
- Next row: Bind off 4 sts, P to end. [3 sts]
- Work 6 rows in st st beg with a K row.
- Bind off.

Version 2

- Cast on 3 sts in dark brown on size 1 (2.25 mm) needles.
- Work 4 rows in st st beg with a K row.
- Next row: Cast on 4 sts, K to end. [7 sts]
- Next row: Cast on 4 sts, P to end. [11 sts]
- Next row: Bind off 4 sts, K to end. [7 sts]
- Next row: Bind off 4 sts, P to end. [3 sts]
- Work 4 rows in st st beg with a K row.
- Next row: Cast on 3 sts, K to end. [6 sts]
- Next row: Cast on 3 sts, P to end. [9 sts]
- Next row: Bind off 3 sts, K to end. [6 sts]
- Next row: Bind off 3 sts, P to end. [3 sts]
- Work 2 rows in st st beg with a K row.
- Bind off.

Version 3

- Cast on 3 sts in dark brown on size 1 (2.25 mm) needles.
- Work 6 rows in st st beg with a K row.
- Next row: Cast on 3 sts, K to end. [6 sts]
- Next row: P.
- Next row: Bind off 3 sts, K to end. [3 sts]
- Next row: Cast on 3 sts, P to end. [6 sts]
- Next row: K.
- Next row: Bind off 3 sts, P to end. [3 sts]
- Work 4 rows in st st beg with a K row.
- Bind off.

Version 4

- Cast on 3 sts in dark brown on size 1 (2.25 mm) needles.
- Work 4 rows in st st beg with a K row.
- Next row: Cast on 2 sts, K to end. [5 sts]
- Next row: Cast on 2 sts, P to end. [7 sts]
- Next row: Bind off 2 sts, K to end. [5 sts]
- Next row: Bind off 2 sts, P to end. [3 sts]
- Work 2 rows in st st beg with a K row.
- Next row: Cast on 2 sts, K to end. [5 sts]
- Next row: Cast on 2 sts, P to end. [7 sts]
- Next row: Bind off 2 sts, K to end. [5 sts]
- Next row: Bind off 2 sts, P to end. [3 sts]
- Work 4 rows in st st beg with a K row.
- Bind off.

Making up

Fold the head and body piece together with the right sides out. Join the front and back neck seams and the underside seams of the body using mattress stitch. Leave the back end open for stuffing. Stuff firmly and close the opening.

With the leg pieces right sides together, oversew the foot part. Turn the legs the right side out and sew the main seams using mattress stitch. Fasten the legs to the sides of the reindeer. The seams should run along the front of the back legs and to the inside of the front legs.

Fold the tail piece in half lengthwise so that the purl side (normally the wrong side) of the knitting is on the outside. Oversew the two long sides together, then stitch the tail in position.

To make up the antlers, with the right sides out, oversew the edges of the vertical and horizontal parts. The piece will tend to fold inward slightly at this stage, but it doesn't matter. Bend the horizontal parts of the antler up slightly and stitch in place by working a couple of stitches in and out of the antler.

To give the reindeers a quirky look, we have embroidered them with slightly different features. You can experiment to find the looks you like best or choose a selection of the following ideas to create a variety of looks.

The basic eye is made from a French knot using black yarn, surrounded by a ring of chain stitch using cream yarn. To make the eyes slightly different, some have a second ring of chain stitch worked around them in either cream or gray/brown yarn. In other cases, the ring of chain stitch is worked in a slightly different shape. One also has an eyelid made from a small spiral of gray/brown chain stitch.

The mouths are embroidered in pink, red, or mauve yarns, using either a straight stitch or a short row of chain stitch. You can add teeth using chain stitch embroidered in white yarn.

The noses are made from a small circle of chain stitch embroidered in black yarn. One reindeer also has a ring of cream yarn embroidered around the nose.

Sew the ears and antlers in position, using the photographs as a guide.

The moon

Casting a magical glow over all the excitement is a beautiful fingernail moon.

Sides
Make 2
• Cast on 14 sts in pale yellow.
• 1st row: P.
• Next row: K1, m1, K to last st, m1, K1. [16 sts]
• Next row: P.
• Rep last 2 rows four times more. [24 sts]
• Next row: K1, m1, K8, bind off 6 sts, K to last st, m1, K1.
• Work on last 10 sts only, leaving other sts on needle.
• Next row: P.
• Next row: k2tog, K to end.
• Next row: P.
• Rep last 2 rows three times more. [6 sts]
• Next row: k2tog, K2, ssk. [4 sts]
• Next row: P.
• Next row: k2tog, ssk. [2 sts]
• Next row: P.
• Next row: k2tog.
• Break yarn and pull yarn end through rem st.

• With ws facing you, join yarn at inner edge of rem 10 sts on needle.
• Next row: P.
• Next row: K to last 2 sts, k2tog.
• Next row: P.
• Rep last 2 rows three times more. [6 sts]
• Next row: k2tog, K2, k2tog. [4 sts]
• Next row: P.
• Next row: (k2tog) twice. [2 sts]
• Next row: P.
• Next row: k2tog.
• Break yarn and pull yarn end through rem st.

Nose
Make 1
• Cast on 8 sts in pale yellow.
• Work 2 rows in st st beg with a K row.
• Next row: K6, turn.
• Leave rem 2 sts on needle and P 6 sts just knitted.
• Work 2 rows in st st across all 8 sts beg with a K row.
• Bind off.

Scarf
• Cast on 4 sts in red.
• K 2 rows.
• Leave red yarn at side and join turquoise yarn.
• K 2 rows.
• Continue in this pattern until the scarf is 9 in/23 cm long, ending with two rows in red.
• Bind off and weave in yarn tails.

Making up
Join the two moon pieces together. With right sides together, use overstitch for the curved sections and, with the right sides out, use mattress stitch for the straight sections. Leave a gap at the front for turning and stuffing. Stuff the moon and sew the gap closed, using mattress stitch.

Sew the nose in place, one side at a time, pinching the nose together before securing the second side. Oversew the top and bottom of the nose.

Using black yarn, embroider two French knots, one on each side, for the eyes. Using cream yarn, work a ring of chain stitch around each French knot. For the mouth, using bright pink yarn, work a straight stitch at each side.

If you wish to hang the moon from your Christmas tree, make a hanging loop by fastening a short length of pale yellow yarn to the top.

As dry leaves before the wild hurricane fly,
When they meet with an obstacle,
mount to the sky,
So up to the house-top the coursers they flew,
With the *sleigh* full of toys, and St. Nicholas too;
And then in a *twinkling*, I heard on the roof,
The prancing and pawing of each little hoof.

As I drew in my *head*, and was turning around,
Down the chimney St. Nicholas came with a bound;
He was dressed all in fur, from his head to his foot,
And his *clothes* were all tarnished with *ashes* and soot;
A bundle of toys was flung on his back,
And he looked like a peddler just *opening* his pack.

Toys & gifts

The waiting and hoping can be the most exciting aspects of Christmas gifts—even better than the gifts themselves. But we hope you'll be thrilled by these presents.

Teddy bear

Legs, body, & head

These are knitted as one piece, from the foot to the top of the head.

Make 1

• Cast on 6 sts in pale brown for the first leg.
• K 12 rows.
• Break yarn and leave sts on needle.
• Cast on 6 sts in pale brown for the second leg.
• K 12 rows.
• Next row: K 6 sts from second leg, K 3 sts from first leg, leave last 3 sts from first leg on small safety pin, and turn.
• Next row: K to last 3 sts, turn and leave these 3 sts on small safety pin.
• Next row: K1, m1, K to last st, m1, K1. [8 sts]
• Next row: K.
• Rep last 2 rows once more. [10 sts]

• K 8 rows.
• Next row: K1, (k2tog) 4 times, K1. [6 sts]
• Next row: K.
• Next row: (K1, m1) 5 times, K1. [11 sts]
• K 7 rows.
• Next row: (k2tog) twice, K3, (k2tog) twice. [7 sts]
• Next row: k2tog, K3, k2tog. [5 sts]
• Bind off.

Transfer sts on pins onto needle so that the outer part of the legs are folded toward the center.

• 1st row: K.
• Next row: K1, m1, K to last st, m1, K1. [8 sts]
• Next row: K.
• Rep last 2 rows once more. [10 sts]
• K 8 rows.
• Next row: K1, (k2tog) 4 times, K1. [6 sts]
• Next row: K.
• Next row: (K1, m1) 5 times, K1. [11 sts]
• K 7 rows.
• Next row: (k2tog) twice, K3, (k2tog) twice. [7 sts]
• Next row: k2tog, K3, k2tog. [5 sts]
• Bind off.

Arms

Make 2

• Cast on 6 sts in pale brown.
• K 10 rows.
• Bind off.

YOU WILL NEED

FOR THE TEDDY BEAR

✳ Small amount of pale brown sport-weight yarn

✳ Small amount of red DK yarn

✳ Very small amount of black DK yarn

✳ 1/8 oz/5 g polyester filling

FOR THE DOLL

✳ Small amounts of bright pink, pale pink, flesh and yellow DK yarn

✳ Very small amounts of black and red DK yarn

✳ 1/8 oz/5 g polyester filling

FOR THE CANDY CANE

✳ Small amounts of red and cream DK yarn

✳ A 3 in/7.5 cm length of plastic-coated wire

FOR THE PRESENTS

✳ Small amount of DK yarn in a color of your choice

✳ Small amount of polyester filling

✳ Length of embroidery floss in a color of your choice

✳ A small button, gold bell, or other decoration

Size 2 (2.75 mm) needles

Size D-3 (3.25 mm) or similar crochet hook

Ears

Make 2

• Cast on 4 sts in pale brown.
• K 2 rows
• Next row: (k2tog) twice. [2 sts]
• Next row: (K1, inc1) twice. [4 sts]
• K 2 rows
• Bind off.

Scarf

Make 1

- Cast on 2 sts in red.
- Work in garter stitch until scarf measures 5 in (13 cm).
- Bind off.

Making up

With the right sides out, oversew the side and top seams of the body and head and the inside leg seams, leaving a gap in the leg seams for stuffing. Stuff and oversew the gap closed. Sew the side seams and lower seams of the two arm pieces and sew the arms in place. Fold the ears in half, oversew around them, and sew them in position.

Using black yarn, embroider two French knots for the eyes and one French knot for the nose. Also using black yarn, make an upside down V shape for the mouth.

Doll

Body & head

The striped leotard and head are knitted as one piece, from the base of the leotard to the top of the head.

Make 2

- Cast on 7 sts in bright pink.
- Work 2 rows in st st beg with a K row.
- Leave bright pink yarn at side and join pale pink yarn.
- Using pale pink yarn, work 2 rows in st st, beg with a K row.
- Leave pale pink yarn at side.
- Using bright pink yarn, work 2 rows in st st beg with a K row.
- Leave bright pink yarn at side.
- Using pale pink yarn, work 2 rows in st st beg with a K row.

- Break pale pink yarn.
- Using bright pink yarn, work 2 rows in st st beg with a K row.
- Break bright pink yarn and join flesh yarn.
- Next row: K.
- Next row: p2tog, P3, p2tog. [5 sts]
- Next row: (K1, m1) 4 times, K1. [9 sts]
- Work 5 rows in st st beg with a P row.
- Next row: (k2tog) twice, K1, (ssk) twice. [5 sts]
- Next row: p2tog, P1, p2tog. [3 sts]
- Next row: sl1, k2tog, psso. [1 st]
- Break yarn and pull it through rem st.

Legs

Make 2

- Cast on 5 sts in flesh.
- Work 10 rows in st st beg with a K row.
- Bind off.

Arms

Make 2

- Cast on 4 sts in flesh.
- Work 10 rows in st st beg with a K row.
- Bind off.

Skirt

Make 1 piece

- Cast on 19 sts in bright pink.
- Work 6 rows in st st beg with a K row.
- Next row: (K1, k2tog) 6 times, K1. [13 sts]
- Bind off.

Making up

With right sides of the head and body pieces together, oversew around the leotard sides and head in matching yarns, leaving the lower edge open for turning and stuffing. Turn the piece the right sides out, stuff, and then sew the gap closed. With the right sides out, sew the seam on the arms and legs using mattress stitch and sew them in position. Sew the back seam of the skirt and oversew in place. Using black yarn, embroider two French knots for the

eyes. Using red yarn, work a straight stitch for the mouth. For the hair, cut eight 3-in (8-cm) lengths of yellow yarn and stitch in place at the top and sides of the head. Use a red crayon to color the cheeks.

Candy cane

- Cast on 22 sts in red.
- 1st row: K.
- Join cream yarn and K 1 row.
- Bind off.

Curl the piece of knitting around the wire and oversew in place. Bend over the top of the cane to form a handle.

Present

Make 1

- Cast on 8 sts in DK yarn.
- K 12 rows.
- Next row: Cast on 5 sts, K to end. [13 sts]
- Next row: Cast on 5 sts, K to end. [18 sts]
- K 12 rows.
- Next row: Bind off 5 sts, K to end. [13 sts]
- Next row: Bind off 5 sts, K to end. [8 sts]
- K 20 rows.
- Bind off.

Making up

Fold the corners upwards to form a lidded box shape, with the right side on the inside. Oversew the short vertical sides and two sides of the "lid." Turn the right way out, stuff lightly, and sew the gap closed.

For the cord, use the crochet hook and embroidery floss to make an 8-in (20-cm) crochet chain. Tie the cord around the present and secure in place. Sew the decoration on top.

His eyes—how they twinkled! His dimples how merry!
His cheeks were like roses, His nose like a cherry!
His droll little mouth was drawn up like a bow,
And the beard of his chin was as white as the snow.
The stump of a pipe he held tight in his teeth,
And the smoke it encircled his head like a wreath;

He had a broad face
and a little round *belly*,
That shook when he laughed,
like a bowlful of jelly.

He was chubby and plump, a right *jolly* old elf,
And I *laughed* when I saw him, in spite of myself!
A **wink** of his eye and a *twist* of his **head**,
Soon gave me to know I had nothing to dread.

St. Nicholas

With his generous waistline and advancing years, he doesn't look exactly sprightly. But looks can be deceiving. With his wispy mohair beard, this rosy-cheeked St. Nicholas will be loved by children and soft-hearted grown-ups everywhere.

Doll

Body

The body is worked from the base upward.

Make 2 pieces

* Cast on 20 sts in bright red.
* Work 8 rows in st st beg with a K row.
* Next row: (K2, m1) twice, K to last 4 sts, (m1, k2) twice. [24 sts]
* Next row: K.
* Break bright red yarn and join cream yarn.
* Next row: (K2, m1) twice, K to last 4 sts, (m1, K2) twice. [28 sts]

- Work 25 rows in st st beg with a P row.
- Next row: K2, (k2tog) twice, K to last 6 sts, (ssk) twice, K2. [24 sts]
- Next row: p2tog, P to last 2 sts, p2tog. [22 sts]
- Next row: K2, k2tog, K to last 4 sts, ssk, K2. [20 sts]
- Next row: p2tog, P to last 2 sts, p2tog. [18 sts]
- Next row: K2, k2tog, K to last 4 sts, ssk, K2. [16 sts]
- Next row: p2tog, P to last 2 sts, p2tog. [14 sts]
- Bind off.

Head

The head is worked from the chin to the top of the forehead.

Front

Make 1

- Cast on 14 sts in beige.
- 1st row: K3, inc1 into next st, K to last 4 sts, inc1 into next st, K3. [16 sts]
- Next row: P.
- Next row: K2, m1, K1, m1, K to last 3 sts, m1, K1, m1, K2. [20 sts]
- Next row: P.
- Next row: K2, m1, K to last 2 sts, m1, K2. [22 sts] *
- Work 7 rows in st st beg with a P row.
- Next row: K10, K into f and b of next 2 sts, turn and P4, turn again and K to end. [24 sts]
- Next row: P10, (p2tog) twice, P10. [22 sts]
- Next row: K9, k2tog, ssk, K9. [20 sts]
- Next row: P.
- Next row: K2, k2tog, K to last 4 sts, ssk, K2. [18 sts]
- Next row: p2tog, P to last 2 sts, p2tog. [16 sts]
- Next row: K2, k2tog, K to last 4 sts, ssk, K2. [14 sts]
- Next row: p2tog, P to last 2 sts, p2tog. [12 sts]
- Next row: K2, k2tog, K to last 4 sts, ssk, K2. [10 sts]
- Bind off pwise.

Back

Make 1

- Work as for front as far as *.
- Work 11 rows in st st beg with a P row.
- Next row: K2, (k2tog) twice, K to last 6 sts, (ssk) twice, K2. [18 sts]
- Next row: p2tog, P to last 2 sts, p2tog. [16 sts]
- Next row: K2, k2tog, K to last 4 sts, ssk, K2. [14 sts]
- Next row: p2tog, P to last 2 sts, p2tog. [12 sts]
- Next row: K2, k2tog, K to last 4 sts, ssk, K2. [10 sts]
- Bind off pwise.

Eyes

Make 2

- Cast on 3 sts in cream using size 1 (2.25 mm) needles.
- 1st row: Inc1 into first st, K to last st, inc1 into next st. [5 sts]
- Next row: P.
- Next row: k2tog, K1, ssk. [3 sts]
- Next row: sl1 pwise, p2tog, psso. [1 st]
- Break yarn and pull it through rem st.

Beard

Make 1

- Cast on 30 sts in white mohair or mohair/silk using size 1 (2.25 mm) needles.
- K 2 rows.
- Next row: Bind off 7 sts, K5 (including st on needle after bind-off), bind off 6 sts, K to end. [17 sts]
- Next row: Bind off 7 sts, K5 (including st on needle after bind-off), cast on 6 sts, K to end. [16 sts]
- K 2 rows.
- Next row: k2tog, K to last 2 sts, k2tog. [14 sts]
- K 4 rows.
- Rep last 5 rows five times more. [4 sts]
- Next row: (k2tog) twice. [2 sts]
- Next row: k2tog. [1 st]
- Break yarn and pull it through rem st.

Arms

The arms are knitted from the top of the arm to the tip of the hand.

Make 2

- Cast on 13 sts in cream.
- Work 9 rows in st st beg with a K row.
- Next row: K
- Break cream yarn and join beige yarn.
- Work 18 rows in st st beg with a K row.
- Next row: K6, K into f and b of next st, turn and P2, turn again and K to end. [14 sts]
- Next row: P6, p2tog, P6. [13 sts]
- Work 2 rows in st st beg with a K row.
- Next row: K1, k2tog, K to last 3 sts, ssk, K1. [11 sts]
- Next row: p2tog, P to last 2 sts, p2tog. [9 sts]
- Bind off.

Legs & feet

These are worked from the feet upward.

Make 2

- Cast on 26 sts in beige.
- Work 6 rows in st st beg with a K row.
- Next row: K6, bind off 14 sts, K to end. [12 sts]
- Work 3 rows in st st beg with a K row.
- Break beige yarn and join bright red yarn.
- K 2 rows.
- Work 8 rows in st st beg with a K row.
- Bind off.

Making up

Place the two head pieces right sides together and oversew around the head, leaving the lower edge open. Turn right side out and stuff fairly firmly, then close the opening.

Join the sides and top edge of the body using mattress stitch, leaving the lower edge open. Stuff the doll quite firmly to make sure the stomach is nice and rounded, and close the opening.

Fold the leg pieces lengthwise so the right side is on the inside. Oversew the lower, back, and top seams of the feet. Turn the pieces the right way out and sew the back seams using mattress stitch. Stuff the legs and feet.

Fold the arm pieces lengthwise so the right side is on the inside. Oversew around the hand. Turn the pieces the right way out and sew the arm seams using mattress stitch. The arms do not need to be stuffed.

Join the arms to the body just below the shoulders. Join the legs to the outside edges of the lower edge of the body.

Oversew the head to the body, so that the chin comes about ¾ in/2 cm down from the top edge of the neck.

Oversew the small cream eye circles in place, using the photograph as a guide. Embroider French knots in the center of each eye using black DK yarn. Oversew the beard in place, using the photograph as a guide. Work the mouth in chain stitch, using deep mauve DK yarn. Use a red crayon to color the cheeks and nose.

Sweater

The vest pieces are knitted from the neck edge to the lower edge.

Back

Make 1
- Cast on 20 sts in bright red.
- Work 2 rows in st st beg with a K row.
- Next row: K2, m1, K to last 2 sts, m1, K2. [22 sts]
- Next row: P.
- Rep last 2 rows four times more. [30 sts]
- Place a thread marker at each end of last row.
- Work 8 rows in st st beg with a K row.
- Next row: K5, k2tog, K16, ssk, K5. [28 sts]
- Next row: P.
- Next row: (K2, m1) 13 times, K2. [41 sts]
- Work 11 rows in st st beg with a P row.
- Break bright red yarn and join fluffy white yarn.
- K 3 rows.
- Bind off.

Left front

Make 1
- Cast on 11 sts in bright red.
- Work 2 rows in st st beg with a K row.
- Next row: K1, m1, K to end. [12 sts]
- Next and every ws row: P to last st, K1.
- Rep last 2 rows four times more. [16 sts]
- Place a thread marker at beg of last row.
- Next row: K1, m1, K to end. [17 sts]
- Next row: P to last st, K1.
- Rep last 2 rows once more. [18 sts]
- Next row: K.
- Next row: P to last st, K1.
- Rep last 2 rows once more.
- Next row: (K3, ssk) 3 times, K3. [15 sts]
- Next row: P to last st, K1.
- Next row: (K2, m1) 7 times, K1. [22 sts]
- Next and every ws row: P to last st, K1.
- Work 10 rows in st st beg with a K row and working a K st at end of every ws row.
- Break bright red yarn and join fluffy white yarn.
- K 3 rows.
- Bind off.

Right front

Make 1
- Cast on 11 sts in bright red.
- Work 2 rows in st st beg with a K row.
- Next row: K to last st, m1, K1. [12 sts]
- Next and every ws row: K1, P to end.
- Rep last 2 rows four times more. [16 sts]
- Place a thread marker at end of last row.
- Next row: K to last st, m1, K1. [17 sts]
- Next row: K1, P to end.
- Rep last 2 rows once more. [18 sts]
- Next row: K.
- Next row: K1, P to end.
- Rep last 2 rows once more.
- Next row: (K3, k2tog) 3 times, K3. [15 sts]
- Next row: K1, P to end.
- Next row: K1, (m1, K2) 7 times. [22 sts]

- Next and every ws row: K1, P to end.
- Work 10 rows in st st beg with a K row and working a K st at beg of every ws row.
- Break bright red yarn and join fluffy white yarn.
- K 3 rows.
- Bind off.

Join both shoulder seams of the sweater using mattress stitch.

Sleeves

Make 2
With the right side of your work facing you and using bright red yarn, pick up and knit 11 sts from one thread marker up to the shoulder seam and another 11 sts from the shoulder seam to the other thread marker.
- Work 19 rows in st st beg with a P row.
- Break bright red yarn and join fluffy white yarn.
- K 2 rows.
- Bind off.

Making up

Join the side and sleeve seams of the sweater using mattress stitch.
- With right sides facing you and using fluffy white yarn, pick up and knit 58 sts up the inside edge of the right front, across the back neck edge, and down the inside edge of the left front.
- K 2 rows.
- Bind off loosely.

Belt

Make 1
- Cast on 55 sts in dark brown.
- K 4 rows.
- Bind off.

To make up, join the two short edges of the belt and sew the button onto the center.

Hat

Make 1

- Cast on 42 sts in fluffy white yarn.
- K 3 rows.
- Break fluffy white yarn and join bright red yarn.
- Work 12 rows in st st beg with a K row.
- Next row: K2, (k2tog, K5) 3 times, K1, (ssk, K5) twice, ssk, K2. [36 sts]
- Work 7 rows in st st beg with a P row.
- Next row: K2, (k2tog, K4) 3 times, (ssk, K4) twice, ssk, K2. [30 sts]
- Work 7 rows in st st beg with a P row.
- Next row: K2, (k2tog, K3) twice, k2tog, K2, (ssk, K3) twice, ssk, K2. [24 sts]
- Work 3 rows in st st beg with a P row.
- Next row: K1, (k2tog, K2) 3 times, (ssk, K2) twice, ssk, K1. [18 sts]
- Next and every ws row: P.
- Next rs row: (k2tog) 9 times. [9 sts]
- Next rs row: (k2tog) twice, K1, (ssk) twice. [5 sts]
- Next rs row: K2tog, K1, ssk. [3 sts]
- Break yarn leaving a long tail and draw yarn through rem sts.

Bobble
Make 1
- Cast on 9 sts in fluffy white yarn.
- K 6 rows.
- Bind off.

Making up

Sew the back seam of the hat using mattress stitch and secure all loose yarn ends in the seam. To make the bobble, thread one yarn tail down one long side and then across one short side of the rectangle. Thread the other tail down the other long side and then the other short side. Pull the threads up and knot them tightly. Fasten the bobble to the tip of hat.

Boots

Make 2
- Cast on 28 sts in dark brown.
- Work 8 rows in st st beg with a K row.
- Next row: K9, bind off 10 sts, K to end. [18 sts]
- Work 11 rows in st st beg with a P row.
- Bind off fairly loosely.

Making up

Fold one piece in half with the right sides together. Oversew the back, lower, and upper seams. Turn the boot the right side out and secure loose yarn ends. Complete the second boot in the same way. Roll down top edges.

Mittens

Make 2
- Cast on 13 sts in leaf green.
- K2 rows.
- Work 4 rows in st st beg with a K row.

- Next row: K6, K into f and b of next st, turn and P2, turn again and K to end. [14 sts]
- Next row: P6, p2tog, P6. [13 sts]
- Work 2 rows in st st beg with a K row.
- Next row: K1, k2tog, K7, ssk, K1. [11 sts]
- Next row: p2tog, P2, sl1 pwise, p2tog, psso, P2, p2tog. [7 sts]
- Bind off.

Making up

With the right sides of the mittens together, oversew the side and top seams. Turn the mittens the right side out and secure loose yarn ends.

Sack

The sack is knitted from the top edge to the bottom edge.
Make 2
- Cast on 18 sts in caramel.
- K2 rows.
- Work 24 rows in st st beg with a K row.
- Next row: K3, k2tog, K to last 5 sts, ssk, K3. [16 sts]
- Next row: P.
- Next row: K2, k2tog, K to last 4 sts, ssk, K2. [14 sts]
- Next row: p2tog, P to last 2 sts, p2tog. [12 sts]
- Bind off.

Sack tie

Use the crochet hook and olive green yarn to make a 12-in (30-cm) crochet chain.

Making up

Join the side and bottom seams of the sack using mattress stitch. Starting at the top of one of the side seams, thread the chain along the entire top edge of the sack using large running stitches. Adjust the cord so that the two ends are even and join the ends to the lower edge of the same side seam.

He spoke not a *word*,
but went straight to his work,
And filled all the stockings;
then turned with a jerk,

And laying his *finger*
aside of his nose,
And giving a nod, up the
chimney he rose;
He sprang to his sleigh,
to his team gave a whistle,
And *away they all flew*
like the down of a thistle,

B ut I *heard* him exclaim,
'ere he drove out of sight—
"*Happy Christmas* to all,
and to all a *good night.*"

Christmas wreath

Christmas wreaths are a hugely popular part of the festive season, and we hope this knitted version will be no exception.

YOU WILL NEED

FOR THE WREATH BASE

✳ 1 oz/30 g (90 yds/82 m) of mid green DK yarn

✳ ¼ oz/7 g (20 yds/18 m) of lime green DK yarn

✳ ¼ oz/7 g (20 yds/18 m) of dark green DK yarn

✳ A ring shape cut from ¼-in/5-mm thick foam board. The ring should measure 10¼ in/26 cm in diameter from the outside edges. The hole should measure 8 in/20 cm in diameter.

✳ 1 oz/30 g polyester filling

FOR THE DECORATIONS

✳ ⅛ oz/5 g (16 yds/15 m) each of cream, dark red, bright red, mid pink, and bright pink DK yarn

✳ Very small amounts of black and ochre DK yarn

✳ Small amounts of dark green and lime green DK yarn

✳ Small amount of polyester filling

✳ A selection of buttons for the flower centers and the bow center, and for decorating the base of the wreath

✳ A selection of sewing threads

Size 2/3 (3 mm) knitting needles

Size D-3 (3.25 mm) or similar crochet hook

Wreath

Base

Make 1

• Cast on 33 sts in mid-green.
• K 46 rows.
• Break yarn and join lime green yarn.
• K 12 rows.
• Break yarn and join mid green yarn.
• K 54 rows.
• Break yarn and join dark green yarn.
• K 36 rows.
• Break yarn and join mid green yarn.
• K 10 rows.
• Break yarn and join lime green yarn.
• K 24 rows.
• Break yarn and join mid green yarn.
• K 20 rows.
• Bind off.

Making up

Seam the short edges using mattress stitch. Stretch the knitting over the foam ring so the two long edges meet around the ring's center. Oversew the long edges together, stuffing along the foam ring as you go.

Bird

Side 1

Make 1

• Cast on 12 sts in cream.
• 1st row: K1, inc1, K to last 3 sts, inc1, K to end. [14 sts]
• Next row: P.
• Next row: K1, m1, K to last st, m1, K1. [16 sts]
• Next row: P.
• Rep last 2 rows twice more. [20 sts]
• Next row: K1, m1, K to end. [21 sts]
• Next row: P.
• Rep last 2 rows three times more. [24 sts]
• Next row: K1, m1, K5, ssk, bind off 6 sts, K to end.
• Turn and work on 10 sts just knitted only, leaving rem sts on needle.
• Next row: P.
• Next row: K1, k2tog, K to end. [9 sts]
• Work 3 rows in st st beg with a P row.
• Next row: K1, k2tog, K to end. [8 sts]

- Next row: P.
- Next row: K1, k2tog, K2, ssk, K1. [6 sts]
- Next row: P.
- Next row: K1, k2tog, ssk, K1. [4 sts]
- Bind off pwise.
- With ws facing you, join yarn to ws of 8 sts rem on needle.
- Next row: p2tog, P to end. [7 sts]
- Next row: K to last 3 sts, ssk, K1. [6 sts]
- Next row: p2tog, P to end. [5 sts]
- Next row: k2tog, K1, ssk. [3 sts]
- Next row: P.
- Next row: sl1, k2tog, psso. [1 st]
- Break yarn and pull it through rem st.

Side 2
Make 1

- Cast on 12 sts in cream.
- 1st row: K3, inc1, K to last st, inc1, K1. [14 sts]
- Next row: P.
- Next row: K1, m1, K to last st, m1, K1. [16 sts]
- Next row: P.
- Rep last 2 rows twice more. [20 sts]
- Next row: K to last st, m1, K1. [21 sts]
- Next row: P.
- Rep last 2 rows three times more. [24 sts]
- Next row: K10, bind off 7 sts, K to last st, m1, K1.
- Turn and work on last 8 sts only, leaving rem sts on needle.
- Next row: P to last 2 sts, p2tog. [7 sts]
- Next row: K1, k2tog, K to end. [6 sts]
- Next row: P to last 2 sts, p2tog. [5 sts]
- Next row: ssk, K1, k2tog. [3 sts]
- Next row: P.
- Next row: sl1, k2tog, psso. [1 st]
- Break yarn and pull it through rem st.
- With ws facing you, join yarn to ws of 10 sts rem on needle.
- Next row: P.
- Next row: K to last 3 sts, ssk, K1. [9 sts]
- Work 3 rows in st st beg with a P row.
- Next row: K to last 3 sts, ssk, K1. [8 sts]
- Next row: P.
- Next row: K1, k2tog, K2, ssk, K1. [6 sts]
- Next row: P.
- Next row: K1, k2tog, ssk, K1. [4 sts]
- Bind off pwise.

Beak
Make 1

- Cast on 4 sts in ochre.
- K 1 row.
- Next row: (k2tog) twice. [2 sts]
- Next row: k2tog. [1 st]
- Break yarn and pull it through rem st.

Making up

With right sides together, oversew around the edge, leaving a gap for turning and stuffing. Turn right side out and stuff lightly, then close the gap.

Embroider a heart on one side of the bird in chain stitch, using dark red yarn. Using black yarn, embroider a French knot for the eye. Using cream yarn, work a ring of chain stitch around the French knot. Using a separated strand of black yarn, work three straight stitches around the eye for the eyelashes. Fold beak in half and sew it in position.

Flowers

The flowers are made from a series of five petals that are knitted as a strip, then gathered together. Each petal is knitted on a base of three of the cast-on stitches. Make one flower in dark red, one in mid pink, and one in bright pink.

Petals

- Cast on 15 sts in dark red, mid pink, or bright pink.
- 1st row: inc1, K1, inc1. [5 sts]
- Next row: K.
- Next row: inc1, K3, inc1. [7 sts]
- K 7 rows.
- Next row: k2tog, K3, k2tog. [5 sts]
- Next row: K.
- Next row: k2tog, K1, k2tog. [3 sts]
- Bind off.
- Rejoin your yarn to the rem sts on your needle and work the next four groups of three stitches in the same way.

Leaves

Make two pairs in dark green and one pair in lime green. The leaves are knitted from the base to the tip.

- Cast on 2 sts in dark or lime green.
- 1st row: K1, inc1. [3 sts]
- Next row: P.
- Next row: K1, m1, K to last st, m1, K1. [5 sts]
- Next row: P.
- Rep last 2 rows twice more. [9 sts]
- Work 2 rows in st st beg with a K row.
- Next rs row: K1, k2tog, K3, ssk, K1. [7 sts]
- Next and every ws row: P.
- Next rs row: K1, k2tog, K1, ssk, K1. [5 sts]
- Next rs row: k2tog, K1, ssk. [3 sts]
- Next rs row: sl1, k2tog, psso. [1 st]
- Break yarn and pull it through rem st.

Making up

Run one of the yarn tails through the base of all the petals, pull it up, and secure. Thread the yarn tail from the tip of the leaf down the side to the base and use the two yarn tails for sewing the leaves in place.

Cord

Bow

Using one strand of bright red yarn and one strand of lime green yarn, use your crochet hook to make a 12-in (30-cm) chain.

Hanging loop and decorating

Use the crochet hook and bright red yarn to make a 60-inch (150-cm) crochet chain.

Making up the wreath

Sew the flowers and leaves around the wreath and sew the buttons onto the center of the flowers. Wrap the red cord around the top of the wreath to form a hanging loop and wrap the remainder of the cord around the wreath. Sew the bird in place. Arrange the cord for the bow into a bow shape. Sew it in place and add a button to the center. Sew the remaining buttons in place on the wreath base.

Index